D1172151

ORGANIZING ARCHIVAL RECORDS

A Practical Method
of Arrangement and Description
for Small Archives

David W. Carmicheal

Pennsylvania Historical and Museum Commission
Harrisburg, 1993

Copyright © 1993 by David W. Carmicheal

ISBN 0-89271-051-9

❖ ACKNOWLEDGMENTS

I would like to acknowledge the assistance of Frank Suran, Brother Denis Sennett, Kathleen Roe, Barbara Efrat, Diana Maull, and Yvonne Carmicheal for reading the manuscript of this work and making many helpful comments. Frank Suran, in particular, read many drafts, improved the work with insightful suggestions, and encouraged me in numerous ways. I thank them for their help, particularly because a work like this raises theoretical questions on which we can never fully agree. Their willingness to downplay areas of disagreement and help me produce a book which might be of assistance to beginning archivists is greatly appreciated.

David W. Carmicheal

David W. Carmicheal is the County Records Manager and Archivist for Westchester County, New York. He earned his Bachelor of Arts in History and English from Asbury College and his Master of Arts in History and Archives from Western Michigan University. Before assuming his duties at the Westchester Archives, Mr. Carmicheal served as an Assistant Archivist for the Jacob Javits Papers at the State University of New York at Stony Brook. Mr. Carmicheal has presented a number of workshops on organizing archival records, of which this publication is an outgrowth.

❖ PREFACE

The staff of the Pennsylvania Historical and Museum Commission's Division of Archival and Records Management Services are being asked to respond to an increasing number of inquiries from small historical repositories regarding the arrangement and description of archives and historical manuscripts. Most often the individuals seeking assistance are relative newcomers to the archival profession, having had virtually no experience or training in the administration of historical records. The Commission's usual response to those inquiring has been to invite them to the State Archives at Harrisburg to see how we manage our holdings, to provide them information on professional training opportunities, and if possible to have a staff member visit their institutions. However, in many cases, we have wished we could refer them to a manual specifically designed to meet their needs as novices in the field. We are pleased to publish this manual by David W. Carmicheal because we believe it helps to fill a void in existing archival literature. Though manuals are not a substitute for supervised on-the-job training at an established archival repository, we think this publication will prove invaluable to institutions that do not have experienced staff and who lack the funds to provide adequate training for new employees. In particular, we recommend this manual be used in conjunction with *Guidelines for Arrangement and Description of Archives and Manuscripts,* which was prepared by Kathleen D. Roe for use in the New York Documentary Heritage Program, and Fred Miller's Society of American Archivists manual titled *Arranging and Describing Archives and Manuscripts.* Complete citations for these and other publications appear in the bibliography.

Brent D. Glass
Executive Director

❖ CONTENTS

Acknowledgments   iii

Preface   v

Introduction   ix

Purpose of Organization   1

Levels of Organization   3

Steps of Organization   11

Conclusion   32

Appendix

    Record and Manuscript Groups   33

    Exercises and Answers   36

    Bibliography   50

Index   51

Cover photo courtesy of The State Museum of Pennsylvania

Photo: Diana Maull

❖ INTRODUCTION

This manual is designed for the person who has little or no formal training in archival work, but who is responsible for the care of historical records. You may work in a historical society, religious institution or school, a municipal government or library; you may be a volunteer or a paid employee to whom the care of historical records has been assigned as an adjunct duty. You may be doing this job out of zeal for the cause of history or simply because your boss has thrown it in your lap. Whatever your situation, this manual is intended to make your job a little easier.

This manual will show you one way to arrange and describe the documents in your care. It begins by telling you a little of the theory behind archival arrangement and description, then it describes a simple step-by-step method to arrange and describe archival records and historical manuscripts. Readers should not think that the method represented here is the only way to arrange and describe historical records. It is one way which has proved practical. The steps described here are not suited to every imaginable situation you may encounter, but they were worked out over several years in consultation with local historians, town clerks and librarians, and they are applicable to the majority of records encountered in their collections.

The best way to use this manual is to read it all the way through and do the written exercises. **It is important that you complete each exercise because the answers often contain new information which could not be conveniently included in the main text.** Once you have finished your first reading, select a collection of records from your own archives and follow the step-by-step instructions found in Chapter 3 until you have arranged and described that one collection. After that, repeat the steps in Chapter 3 for each of your collections.

❖ PURPOSE OF ORGANIZATION

The main purpose of arrangement and description is to get a researcher from his or her question to the answer which may be found in your records. The question may be as simple as "who was the first mayor of our town?" or as complex as "how did the people of our town live in the early nineteenth century?" but in each case, how you arrange and describe your materials will determine whether, and how quickly, you will be able to assist the researcher.

You have probably used a library on many occasions. Perhaps with the help of a reference librarian you have found the answer to a question simply by locating an appropriate book, glancing at the index, and turning to the proper page. Like libraries, archives are sources of information; but unlike books, archival materials are rarely indexed or arranged in anything approaching a comprehensive system.* This difference affects the way archival material is used, and how it is arranged and described. Consider two ways in which books and archival materials differ:

♦ **Intent of Creation:** Books are created to be read. The author of a book about town government hopes that people will read the book and learn more about that subject, so that the needs of the reader are always present in the mind of the author. Archival materials, which are used by researchers, are not created with researchers in mind. They are, in fact, by-products of day-to-day human activity. The first mayor of your town, writing to commend a member of the community for initiative in starting a civic group, did not consider that researchers might one day come into your archives to use his letter for historical research — the record was created simply in connection with his daily activities and was intended only for a particular reader. The same is true of all archival records — the people who created them did not create them for the convenience of historians and researchers. Since archival records are not created with researchers in mind, they tend to differ from books in another respect:

♦ **Specificity of Subject:** A book usually is about a single subject. The author who wants to sell books would not set out to write a book about town government and then digress for a chapter to discuss the effect of the moon on tides. People who create archival records have no such limitations. The correspondence files of a mayor, for example, may cover a wide range of topics, from drug education, to crowning the winner of the local beauty pageant, to installing traffic lights. All of this means that books in a library may be classified — that

---

*You probably accompanied the librarian into the stack area to look for the book. Archival storage areas, unlike those in most libraries, are usually off limits to the public; this makes your arrangement and description even more important because the researcher cannot browse your shelves to find materials.

is, a book about town government may be placed with other books about town government or government in general — but archival materials are not easy to classify because they usually deal with more than one subject.

What all this means is that archival materials cannot be arranged and described in the same way as books. Consider, for example, a researcher who wants to know when James Harrow was mayor of your town. He or she may visit the local library, locate a book entitled *Mayors of the Town,* and find "Harrow, James" in the index. If no book has been written and the archives are consulted, however, the researcher may need to sift through a large collection of records entitled "James Harrow Papers" to locate the information. How the records have been arranged and described will determine whether the researcher must search the entire collection or a small portion of it.

The emphasis in archival arrangement and description is to narrow the search to a small portion of a large collection. If the James Harrow Papers have been arranged and described properly, chances are good that the records related to his term as mayor will be separate from those of his business, his work with the Boy Scouts, and his personal activities. The researcher may not be able to lay hands on a specific piece of information in a matter of minutes, but the arrangement and description of the records will make it obvious where the answer is most likely to be found.

Do not think that you must index every item in your archives — leave that to the book writers! Arrange and describe carefully and you should be able to determine where the answer to a question is most likely to be found. Keep in mind that your primary job is to **narrow the search.**

Before you can begin the step-by-step arrangement and description of your records, you need to know certain terms which are defined in the next section, "Levels of Organization."

❖ LEVELS OF ORGANIZATION

In the last section we compared archival records to library materials. We will begin this section with one more comparison. Librarians usually arrange and describe at the book level. In other words, it is the individual books which are arranged on the shelves in relation to one another and which are described in the card catalog. Archivists, on the other hand, may arrange and describe on several levels. One key to good description is to describe each collection at a level appropriate to the records themselves. In this manual we will discuss only two levels of arrangement and description: the collection level and the series level. These terms are described in this section along with a third term, "accessions."

❖ Collections

Every archives is made up of collections. If your archives houses the papers of the town's founding family (named Foundling) they are the "Foundling Family Papers" — one collection in your archives. If you have the records of a local railroad company, they are another collection: the "Magnate Railroad Company Records." **Each forms a "collection" because each is made up of documents which were created or compiled by a single source** — an individual, family, organization, government, office, business or other entity.*

A collection may (and probably will) include many types of documents. "The Foundling Family Papers," for example, may include correspondence, diaries, photographs and scrapbooks. All of these form one collection, however, because they were created or compiled by the same family or individual. In the same way, the "Magnate Railroad Company Records" probably include correspondence, invoices, receipts, and even maps and photographs. Again, these various items form a single collection because they were created or compiled by the same organization or business.

Normally the identity of the creator or compiler of a collection is obvious; but sometimes you must examine the records carefully to discover this information. To take an extreme example, an archivist looking at an autograph collection might mistake it at first glance for a collection of correspondence. The fact that these documents were brought together because of their signatures might become apparent only after closer examination. Such a collection would be treated as the autograph collector's collection since he or she compiled it. This does not happen frequently in small collections, but you should be aware of the possibility. What happens more frequently is that a collection may seem, at first

---

*For a discussion of other terms used by archivists, see Appendix, p. 33.

glance, to have been created by an entire family when, in fact, it was compiled by a single member of that family. The collection may contain letters, for example, which bear the names of various family members; but they may have been received by one person (and thus "compiled" by that person). The collection, then, is the collection of the one person who compiled it, rather than of the entire family.

Finally, it is possible that you will be unable to determine the creator or compiler of some collections. In this case you should do one of two things: you may name the collection for the person most closely associated with the records. For instance, if you have a collection of photographs of Jill Simpson and you don't know who collected them, name them the "Jill Simpson Collection" since she is the person most closely associated with the collection. Another option is to name the collection for the place or activity to which the records relate. If you have a group of early playbills (programs) from the Centerville Little Theater which some unknown person donated to the archives long ago, call it the "Centerville Little Theater Collection" since it relates to that particular place.

Determining the creator or compiler of a collection of records is obviously important. Before you go on, look at Exercise A (exercises and answers begin on page 36). It will help you learn more about the concept of collections.

❖ Series

A series is **part** of a collection. You might say that series are the building blocks of collections. If you examined the records of the "Magnate Railroad Company" closely, you might discover that the records fall naturally into distinct groups. Some of the records might be "accounts payable" — ledgers indicating money owed by the company to others. Other records might be of "property" — records of buildings and land owned by the company. Still other records might be "personnel files," documenting each employee in the company. Each of these sets of records forms one series. **A series is a group of records kept together because they all relate to the same activity.**

A more formal way to state this is to say that a series is a body of documents or file units that was consciously created or filed in a certain way to enable one to carry out a particular function. In simpler terms, **all of the records in a single series have the same function.** Notice that the accounts payable ledgers form one series because they all have a single function: to indicate how much money the company owes and to whom. Likewise, the property records form one series because they too have a single function: to document the land owned by the company along its railroad routes. The personnel files also form one series, because these records all serve the function of documenting the employees who work for the company.

To take another example, the "Foundling Family Papers" may consist of three series as well. Certain records, for instance, may pertain to the family business;

others may relate to Mr. Foundling's term as mayor of the town; a third series of records may document Mrs. Foundling's activities as founder of the local YWCA. Each series of records relates to a single activity.

Notice that nothing has been said here about the form of the records. For instance, the accounts payable records mentioned above may have come to your archives as loose files, bound volumes, index cards, or a combination of all three. In fact, the records in one series may be totally dissimilar in format; but if they all have the same function, they are a series. To look at it another way, it is easy to imagine that the personnel files series might include a variety of documents which appear, at first glance, to have nothing in common: employment applications, medical release forms and various test results, to name a few. But, again, these various records serve a single function — to document the employees of the company. That ties them together and makes them a series.

A series is not normally something you create in a collection, rather it is something you **discover** in a collection — it is already there. In fact, what you are really trying to discover is **how the documents were grouped when they were being used by the people who created or compiled them.** Since people tend to group their documents by function, the best way to discover how the records were originally maintained by their creators is to determine which records serve the same function. Sometimes it is difficult to tell whether records serve the same function, but there are several clues to look for:

♦ **Clue 1: Filing Systems:** Records which function together are usually filed together in some systematic way. The personnel files would probably come to your archives together in a recognizable filing arrangement, perhaps chronological (by date of employment) or alphabetical (by name of employee). The Foundling family business records might include invoices filed together in some filing arrangement (perhaps numerically by invoice number).

♦ **Clue 2: Content:** If you have a group of records which all record the same content — in other words, have the same (or very similar) information — they probably serve the same function. Each accounts payable record probably documents the same kind of information: the name of the vendor, the amount owed, the date paid and other information.

♦ **Clue 3: Format:** This can be a deceptive clue; as we have seen, the records in a single series may come in many formats. But format is sometimes a clue to function nonetheless. For example, someone may donate to your archives a collection of phonograph records which may constitute one series. The key is whether the phonograph records were maintained together by the person who collected them.

All of these are clues, but you can be certain that documents belong together in a series only if they meet the following criteria:

- ◆ They all relate to the same activity or function;
- ◆ There is some possibility that they were maintained together by the person (or organization or office, etc.) who created or compiled them.

You may wonder how many documents are necessary to form one collection or one series? The answer is one. A series might be composed of a single document, and a collection might be composed of just one series. In particular, collections of individuals and families often consist of a single series because individuals do not always file their records as carefully as do organizations. Normally, though, there are many records in each series and several series in each collection. Exercise B (page 39) will help you learn to identify series in a collection. After you have finished the exercise you will study the term "accessions."

Photographs can be an important element of family collections. *(Photo: Pennsylvania State Archives)*

❖ Accessions

An accession is a **group of records donated or otherwise transferred to your archives together.** Simply put, any records which come in the door together form a single accession. If Mrs. Jones walks in and donates three boxes of records, these constitute one accession. (Of course, the archives should take legal, as well as physical, custody of all accessions, but that issue is not within the scope of this manual.) **In most small archives, each accession is also one collection.** That is, Mrs. Jones's three boxes probably contain records created by a single individual or group. (It could be that the archives already has records created by this same individual or group, although this is more likely to occur if you collect the records of active businesses or organizations. You will learn later what to do in such cases.)

You may want to stop here and make certain that you are familiar with the terms "collection," "series," and "accession." Exercise C (page 41) will help you.

It is vitally important that you keep track of each new accession as it arrives in the archives. Follow the steps below to register each. This section will also tell you what to do with records that were already in the archives before you read this manual.

❖ Registering Each Accession

❖ Complete an Accession Sheet

The form shown in Figure 1 (page 8) is an "accession sheet." You should complete one of these for each new accession the same day the records arrive in your archives.

An accession sheet includes the following:

◆ **Accession Number:** This is a number used to identify the records while they sit on the shelf waiting to be arranged and described. The easiest way to create an accession number is to use the year in which the records came into the archives, followed by a sequential number (e.g., 1990/1 is the first accession to arrive in 1990. The next accession gets the number 1990/2, the third gets 1990/3 and so on until 1991, when you begin again with 1991/1). **Be sure to keep track of which accession number you have reached so you do not assign the same number twice.**

◆ **Title:** Give the records a title which reflects what you know about them. If you know only that they are the papers of a family named Smith, call them the "Smith Family Papers." This is a temporary title and will be changed when you examine the papers more carefully.

◆ **Donor/Office of Origin:** Record the name, address and phone number of the person responsible for transferring these records to the archives. You should also record the donor's relationship to the papers (is he or she the creator or compiler?).

◆ **Date Accessioned:** Record the day, month, and year the records came in the door of the archives.

◆ **Notes:** Use this area for miscellaneous notes about the collection. For example, you may use this space to record the exact location of the boxes if you are unable to place them on the shelf in numerical order. You may also use this space to note how many boxes are in the accession.

You might keep your accession sheets in a three-ring binder, or you might want to keep them in a file drawer with one folder for each accession. Using a file drawer makes sense if you have other paperwork, such as a deed of gift, to keep with the accession sheet.

❖ Label and Shelve the Accession

Once the accession has been registered, place the records into boxes and label each box with the accession number; then place the boxes in an area of the archives reserved for records awaiting arrangement and description. If possible, place accessions in this area in sequence (that is, with accession 1990/1 on the shelf, followed by 1990/2, then 1990/3, etc.). If you cannot do this, the exact temporary location of each accession **must** be noted on its accession sheet in the "notes" section. If you move an accession, don't forget to change its location on the accession sheet.

Accession Number:

Title:

Donor/Office of Origin:

Date Accessioned:

Notes:

Figure 1: Accession Sheet

❖ What to Do with Accessions Which Were Already in the Archives Before You Read This Manual

Registering accessions will be easy from now on because you will do it as soon as records arrive, and there is no danger that the records of one accession will get mixed with those of another accession. What should you do if there are unprocessed records already in the archives which are mixed together?

Be certain to make a careful search for accession records which someone may have kept before you arrived. Such records will help you determine which records came to the archives together. If there are records which you know came in at the same time from one source, gather them together, assign an accession number to them, and register them as though they had just arrived (on the "date accessioned" line put today's date or, if you know it, the actual date the records arrived in the archives).

Once all of the known accessions have been registered you will need to divide the remaining materials into "artificial accessions." This must be done **very carefully** and thoughtfully.

Artificial accessions may not be created without careful attention to an archival principle called "provenance." This principle states that the archivist must **never mix records created or compiled by one individual or group with those created or compiled by another individual or group.** The principle of provenance is **crucial** to all archival thinking and never more so than when you are creating artificial accessions.

Unfortunately, if you are faced with a jumbled mass of records and no documentation about how they came to be in the archives, you must group them together as you believe they might have arrived. Try to group together records which were probably created or compiled by the same person or group. **Since you are creating artificial accessions based on who created or compiled them, you are, in fact, creating artificial collections.** Be sure to note on the accession sheet that **you** created this collection.

You must remember that this step is to be taken **only** if you have records which were not registered when they arrived in the archives — something that should not happen from now on! Remember, too, that the principle of provenance must guide your decisions during this step. Once your records have been divided into accessions, treat each accession as if it had just arrived in your archives. Complete an accession sheet for each one, then label and shelve the records as you would any other accession.

In Exercise D (page 43) you will find an example of records in no discernible order. Take a few minutes to look at them and divide them into artificial accessions. Compare your answers to those shown on pages 44 and 45. If you do not feel comfortable with this step, leave your unregistered records until you can get professional help. For now, just work with records that have come into the archives since you began reading this manual.

Once you have finished dividing all of the records in your archives into accessions, you are ready to begin the practical steps of arranging and describing your records one collection at a time. However, before proceeding to the next section, those who are unfamiliar with archival terminology and methodology should read the Appendix, which begins on page 33. Titled "Record and Manuscript Groups," it clarifies variations on the use of certain terminology in archival and manuscript repositories. This section will be particularly helpful to those who will be using this book in tandem with other archival manuals.

Computers can be a valuable tool for cataloging accessions. *(Photo: Thomas Lee, Metropolitan Transportation Authority, New York)*

❖STEPS OF ORGANIZATION

This section takes you through the process of arrangement and description, step by step. To get the most out of this manual you should read it through one time and complete all of the exercises, then select one accession from your archives and complete Steps 1 through 12 on that one accession. When you complete Step 12, that accession will be arranged and described completely and will be ready for researchers to use. Then you can select another accession and complete Steps 1 through 12 on it. You can work on your accessions in any order you choose (that is, accession 1990/1 does not have to be arranged and described before accession 1990/2). Arrange more important accessions before less important ones — just be certain that once an accession has been arranged and described you note that fact on its accession sheet; otherwise someone may look for the accession in its temporary location and not find it.

♦ **Setting Up:** Select an accession and take it (all of it) to a table large enough on which to spread it out. Don't spread the records out yet, just set them on the table as you found them on the shelf (or near the table if the accession is too large).

A word should be said here about the table you will be using. To protect the records you should place only items on the table which are essential to the arrangement and description process. You should **never,** for example, have food or drink or smoking materials near your archival records. It is also important to use only pencil when working with archival materials; using pencil will insure that if you accidentally mark on something it can be removed easily. Ink can damage certain types of records so send your pens into exile.

As noted earlier the accession you have selected is probably one collection. **From now on we will refer to the records on the table in front of you as a collection.** (It may be easier if you think of the records as an "accession" only while they are on the shelf awaiting arrangement and description. Once you begin arranging and describing them you can refer to them as a "collection.") The instructions which follow assume that you are working with a single collection. If you discover as you work with them that the records were, in fact, created or compiled by more than one person or group, you may have two collections. Don't worry about it. Once you are **certain,** you can separate the two collections and treat them individually. For now, select another accession which you are certain is one collection.

Step 1: Assign a Collection Number

Collections are numbered sequentially (1, 2, 3) as they are arranged and described. The number of the collection should be recorded on the collection description sheet. Keep track of collection numbers you have used and cross-reference them to the accession number assigned to the records earlier.

Example: Figure 2

```
                                        Collection Number:




Collection Title:




Background Note:
```

Figure 2: Collection Description Sheet

❖ **Explanation:** Take a "collection description sheet" like the one shown in Figure 2 and write a "1" in the upper right corner after the words "collection number." Since this is the first collection you will be arranging and describing, it is collection number 1. The next collection you arrange and describe will be collection number 2, and so on. You should keep a log of collection numbers so that you know which numbers have been assigned and which is the next to be used.

You should cross-reference the collection number to the accession number you assigned earlier to these records. The easiest way to do so is to note the collection number(s) on the appropriate accession sheet(s).

Now set the page aside and proceed to Step 2.

Step 2: Examine the Collection

Examine each item in the collection and remove paper clips, acidic paper and other hazardous materials. Take careful notes to be used in Step 3.

❖ **Explanation:** During the initial examination you will look through the records carefully, perhaps even item by item. Throughout this step you must remember to keep everything in the **exact order** in which you find it! Archivists speak of the "sanctity of original order" for very good reasons. As you approach the records, think of yourself as an archaeologist confronted with a pile of rare dinosaur bones. The professional carefully plots the location of each bone in the ground exactly as it is found until the order of the entire skeleton becomes clear. In the same way, the records you examine have a special relationship — even if they look about as orderly as a pile of dinosaur bones right now! This relationship may reveal itself only slowly, so proceed carefully.

Open the first box and remove the first document (or volume or folder or whatever). Lay it on the table in front of you and examine it. When you are finished looking at the first document, turn it face down on the table beside you and examine the second document. Then turn that document face down on top of the first one. Continue doing this until you have looked at everything in the box. (Of course, some large accessions may be highly repetitive and may not require such a detailed examination.) If the documents are in folders, be certain to return the documents to the correct folder. As you examine each document you should do two things:

1. **Perform basic conservation work:** If you have the time to do it you can help preserve the documents if you:

a. Remove all rubber bands and paper clips and, only if they are essential, replace them with plastic paper clips (usually called "plastiklips"). Remove staples only if they are rusted or are damaging the paper in some other way.

b. Look for acidic pieces of paper in the collection. The clue to acidic paper is its color (usually brown), its condition (often brittle), and its effect on surrounding documents (often it "burns" or stains the paper it touches). The most common types of acidic paper are newspaper clippings, carbon copies (press copies), and scraps of paper used as bookmarks. Bookmarks may be discarded or, if their placement is essential to understanding the collection, replaced with acid-free paper. In the case of newspaper clippings and carbon copies (or any other acidic pages you may find) either replace the acidic page with a photocopy or sandwich the original document between sheets of acid-free paper. In either case you will be protecting the rest of the collection from the acid which might migrate from the acidic paper to less acidic pages.

c. Unfold and gently flatten documents which have been bent or rolled. Badly curled documents may require humidification before flattening (for this process see Ritzenthaler, *Archives & Manuscripts: Conservation,* in the bibliography, page 50).

d. Place documents in acid-free folders. Documents which are already in folders should be transferred to acid-free folders in the exact order in which they were kept in their original folders. All of the information on the original folder should be written on the new folder.

2. Take notes to use in your background note: As you look at the records ask yourself important questions such as:

a. Who created or compiled the records? (This may differ from what you originally thought.)

b. What types of records are included in the collection? (Some common types of records are wills, diaries, receipts, etc.)

c. What type of information is recorded in the records?

d. What is the range of dates covered by the records?

e. What is the arrangement of the records?

f. Do the records seem to be complete or are there significant gaps? Why might these have occurred?

Be certain to take good notes since these will form the basis of your work in Step 3.

Step 3: Write a Background Note

Write a note to the researcher explaining who created or compiled the collection, why he/she did so, how the records came to be in your archives, and what relation they have to other records in the archives. Write the note on the collection description sheet.

Example: Figure 3

Collection Number: 1

Collection Title: Foundling Family Papers

Background Note:

In June, 1801, John H. Foundling moved with his wife and seven children from Philadelphia to the banks of the Scrawny River in southeastern Ohio where he founded Middletown. Foundling organized a trading post and began to supply settlers as they moved west via the Scrawny.

By 1844, when Foundling died, Middletown was a thriving town and Foundling's eldest son, John Jr., was mayor. Other family members owned the town's only bank, grocery store and livery stable. Also by that year, Foundling's youngest son, Percival, was famous as a composer (best known for his song, "Way Down Upon the Scrawny River").

The papers in this collection were compiled by John H. Foundling, John Jr., and Percival between 1808 and 1847 and consist mainly of extensive correspondence among the three. They were donated to the archives in 1901 in honor of Middletown's Centennial.

Figure 3: Background Note

❖ **Explanation:** The purpose of background research is to make it possible for you to write what this manual will call a "collection background note." It is usually a short paragraph but, in rare instances, it may be several pages long. The length is not important, the content is.

In the collection background note, you tell the researcher who created or compiled the records, why he/she did so, how the records came to be in your archives and, in general terms, what relation they have (if any) to the rest of the collections in your archives. Remember: if you created the collection artificially you must note that fact here. The type of information you include depends to some extent on whether the records were created or compiled by a public organization or business, or by a private person or family. (Archivists often refer to this note as an "administrative history" if the records were created or compiled by an organization, and a "biographical note" if the creator/compiler was a person or group of individuals.)

If the records were created or compiled by an organization, you should look for the following information:
> date of founding
> reason for existence
> divisions, and date each was founded
> principal officers
> significant events in the life of the organization

If the records were created or compiled by an individual or family, you should look for the following information:
> key dates in the life of the person or group
> various addresses
> types of work
> interests and activities
> associations and offices

The information for the collection background note may be found in a variety of sources: interviews with the donor; published sources, such as biographical dictionaries; and even in the records themselves. For some collections you will know a great deal; for others you may never learn much of this information. The key is to take whatever you learn and write a paragraph, such as the one shown in Figure 3 (page 15).

Once you have completed the collection background note, proceed to Step 4.

Step 4: Write a Collection Title

Write a title for the collection. The title should include the name of the person, family or organization which created or compiled the records.

Example: Figure 3 (page 15)

❖ **Explanation:** Next you should give the collection a title. Since collections are based on who created or compiled them, this information should always be included in the title. Your title should be descriptive but should not be too long.

Once you have added the title, your collection description sheet is complete. You are ready to work with the series in the collection.

Step 5: Identify Series in the Collection

Group the records in the collection into series and arrange them together on the table.

❖ **Explanation:** By now you have a good idea what your collection contains and the series should be fairly evident. Properly identifying series is crucial because it will determine the final arrangement of your collection (and that, of course, will determine how quickly you are able to locate information in the future). At this point you should identify the series and physically group them together. Discover the series in the collection, don't create them. You are trying to re-create the original arrangement of the records.

Why do archivists insist on re-creating the original order? After all, isn't it much easier just to sort everything by subject? We have already seen that, unlike books, a single archival record may cover a surprising number of subjects. This alone will make subject arrangement difficult and time consuming (and, after all, we are looking for ways to speed up this process). But there are additional reasons for maintaining the original order. To name just two:

♦ **Reason 1:** The possible existence of indexes and other references to the records makes the original order very important. Suppose, for example, you set out to arrange and describe a collection of business records and find that they are in numerical order, but that this order makes it difficult to find the records by the name of the client. You may be tempted to rearrange the records by the name of the client. If you do so you may find, sometime later, that an index to the records has been found which would have allowed you to access the records by the name of the client as well as by the year of the transaction and other such information. It seems to be an archival "Murphy's Law" that if you disturb the original order of records, you will end up re-creating the same order later on — or wishing that you were able to.

♦ **Reason 2:** In order to understand the second reason, you must think about your house. What would happen if you were to rearrange your house so that all of the equipment and supplies you use for washing are in a single room? Such a room might contain your washing machine, your dishwasher, even your bathtub. Or what if you arranged all of the powders in your house in one cupboard? It would contain your laundry powder, a box of powdered milk, and your bath powder. If you were to do so, you would be arranging your house, in effect, by subject.

The reason you would be foolish to arrange your house by subject is that each room in your house is furnished and arranged according to the **activity** which takes place there. You know, for instance, to look for the washer and dryer in the laundry room because both relate to the activity of washing clothes. That, by the way, is why the dirty clothes are in the same room — because they relate to the activity of laundering. The activity to which these items relate is enough (and, in fact, is the only thing) to make sense out of their relationship. Like the rooms in your house, **the records in a collection are arranged in relation to one another on the basis of the activities to which they relate.** If you remove them from that context, they become individual pieces of paper. Like a junked washing machine lying by the road, a piece of paper out of context has no use.

When you have finished arranging and describing this collection, you will have access to it by subject. Instead of arranging the records by subject, however, the archivist creates "finding aids" or subject indexes which help the researcher locate all records pertaining to a given subject. These will be discussed in greater detail in Step 12.

At the conclusion of this step you will probably have several piles of records (series) on the table in front of you or on nearby shelving — whichever is more convenient. Refer to page 4 if you need help discovering the series in a collection.

Step 6: Arrange the Records Within Each Series

Arrange the records in the series in some logical manner (chronological, alphabetical, etc.). Remember that the original order of the records takes precedence over other arrangements.

❖ **Explanation:** Select one of the series in your collection and look at it. The records in this series may already be arranged in some logical manner, perhaps chronologically or alphabetically or numerically. If they are not in order, study them carefully to see whether you can determine their original order (correspondence files, for example, are usually arranged chronologically).

Remember that archivists regard the original order as sacrosanct. If you can determine the original order of the records within a series, it is imperative that you maintain this order. If, after very careful examination, no order can be discerned, place the records in the order in which they most likely would have been kept when they were in active use.

Note that the arrangement of the records has nothing to do with their format. All of the records — loose files, microfilm, bound volumes — should be placed in the proper arrangement without regard to their formats. Once you have determined the arrangement to use, go through the records in this series and physically arrange them on the table in front of you. For instance, if you are arranging correspondence files chronologically, go through all of the correspondence and place it in chronological order at this time. As you place file folders in order you may box them.

After you have finished this series select another and do the same — determine its arrangement and physically arrange it. Continue this until each series in the collection has been arranged properly. Exercise E (page 46) will assist you in this step.

Step 7: Arrange the Series in Relation to One Another

Arrange all of the series in the collection in some logical manner. The series arrangement usually reflects the hierarchy of the system which produced the records.

❖ **Explanation:** The series themselves are next arranged in relation to one another in some logical way. In a business collection a logical arrangement is often easy to discover — invoices might be placed before receipts for example.

In a collection of personal papers (correspondence, diaries, etc.) there may be no obvious relationship among the series. That is okay; just arrange them in some order. Exercise F (page 48) will give you practice doing this.

By the end of this step you should have the records on the table (or shelf or wherever) grouped by series. The records in each series should be in some logical order, likewise the series themselves. In the next step you will number the boxes and volumes in your collection.

Step 8: Number Each Series and Container

Number each series (the collection number + a sequential number) and then each container or item in the series (the series number + a sequential number).

Example: Figures 4-6 (pages 19, 20, 21)

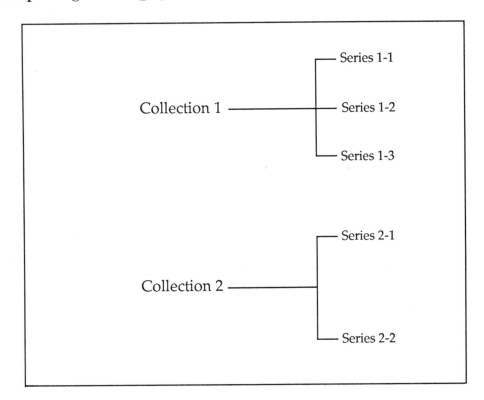

Figure 4: Numbering Series

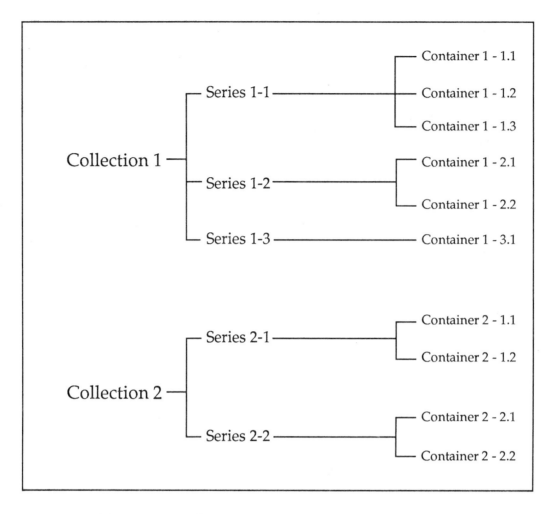

Figure 5: Numbering Series Containers or Items

❖ **Explanation:** Your collection has been arranged into series. Now you can number each series in the collection. The series number is the collection number followed by a dash and then a sequential number, one for each series. Thus, if this is the first series in collection one, its series number is 1-1; if it is the second series in collection one, its series number is 1-2, and so forth. The next collection you work on will be collection 2, so its first series will be 2-1, its second series 2-2, etc. Figure 4 (page 19) illustrates series numbers.

Lastly, number the boxes, volumes or other containers in each series. The first container in series 1-1 gets the number 1 (so that it becomes 1-1.1); the second gets the number 2 (1-1.2) and so on. Figure 5 illustrates container numbers.

You do not need to number each item in each container — only the containers themselves. You may want to number individual maps and photographs if you are going to separate these from your other materials (see Step 10). Whatever you decide to number should be labeled as illustrated in Figure 6 (page 21). Boxes may be numbered using labels (you should use a good label from an archival supplies catalog so that it won't fall off in six months). Bound volumes may be labeled using acid-free strips of paper which stick out of the book like a bookmark. Maps and photographs may be labeled on the reverse of the item. Always use pencil and always put the number in square brackets so that researchers know that it was a number added to the item by someone other than its creator.

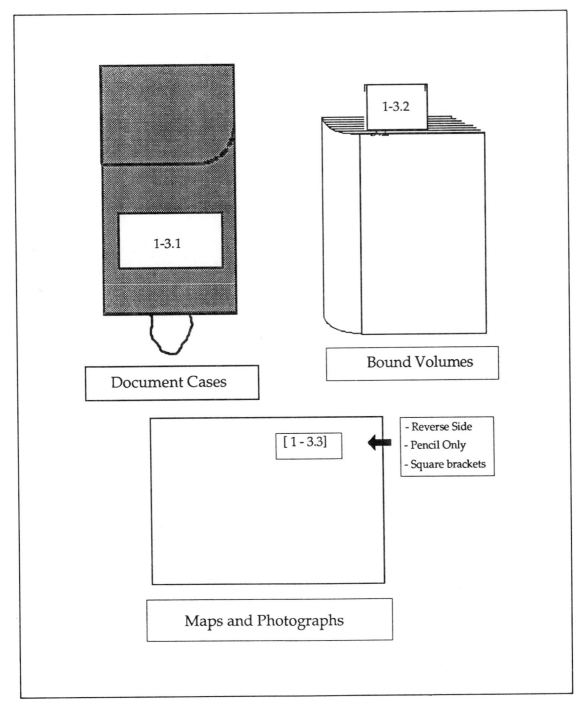

Figure 6: Physically Numbering Containers or Items

Step 9: Complete a Series Description Sheet for Each Series

Complete one series description sheet for each series in the collection.

Example: Figures 7 and 8 (pages 22, 24)

❖ **Explanation:** Now it is time to describe each series in the collection. This is the heart of your work; these are the descriptions your researchers will read to determine whether they want to see the records themselves. A sample series description sheet is shown in Figure 7. You should complete one of these for each series in the collection. A completed form is illustrated in Figure 8 (page 24). The different elements of the series description sheet are described on page 23.

Series Number:

Series Title:

Dates:
Quantity:
Arrangement:

Content Description:

Container List:

Name of Preparer:
Date of Preparation:

Figure 7: Series Description Sheet

- **Series Number:** In this space write the series number which you assigned in Step 8.

- **Series Title:** Write the title which describes this particular series. Just as your collection title needed to include the name of the creator or compiler of the records, your series title needs to include the activity or function which makes these records a series.

- **Dates:** Write the date of the oldest document in the collection and the date of the most recent document (e.g., 1910-1986). The hyphen (-) means "through"; a comma (e.g., 1910, 1986) indicates "and." You may use hyphens and commas in combination. For example, 1910, 1966-1986 means "1910 and 1966 through 1986." In other words, there are no records between 1911 and 1965 in this series.

- **Quantity:** It does not matter how you measure your records as long as you remember two things: use a measurement that anyone can understand (i.e., don't use vague terms like "6 boxes" — how big is a box?), and be consistent. Don't measure some things in linear feet and some in cubic, some in inches and some in centimeters. The easiest way to measure is in linear inches and feet. Simply place the items on a shelf and measure the length of space they take up on the shelf.

- **Arrangement:** Tell how the records in this particular series are arranged. Try to keep this to one word such as "chronological," "alphabetical," or "numerical." Elaborate if you must (e.g., "Chronological and then alphabetical within each year by name of client"), but a one-word summary is usually sufficient.

- **Content Description:** This is the most important description you will write. In it you tell the researcher what you know about the series: what types of records it contains, what activities led to their creation, what information the records give (including what topics and events are represented in the records), what information one might expect them to include which they don't include, and the significant gaps in the records and why these may have occurred. Researchers ought to be able to determine whether they want to look at the actual records by reading the content description. A thorough description will help them narrow their search for information and prevent wasted time and effort.

- **Container List:** This is a list of the parts of the collection (each box, each volume, each reel of microfilm or whatever unit can stand alone). You assigned these numbers at the end of Step 8. An example of a container list is found in Figure 8 (page 24). Note that the parts of the collection have been listed in sequential order without regard to their format. The container list spells out very clearly the arrangement of the series.

❖ **What to do if these records are an addition to a series already in your archives.**

From time to time you will receive records which form part of a series which is already in your archives.* Suppose, for example, you receive a series of birth records from the town clerk's office. You arrange and describe them and

---

Series Number: 1-3

Series Title: Personnel Files

Dates: 1923-1937
Quantity: 1 linear ft.
Arrangement: Alphabetically by name of employee

Content Description:

    Employment applications, references, training certificates, evaluations, and job descriptions for hourly employees of the Magnate Railroad Company.

Container List:

    1-3.1   Abbot, George - Kristen, Marilyn

    1-3.2   Korcoran, William - Peterson, Mark

    1-3.3   Pincher, Penny - Zana, Gerbo

Name of Preparer: Betty Renino
Date of Preparation: 6/16/90

Figure 8: Completed Series Description Sheet

---

* Note that this refers to records which form part of an existing **series**. If you are an institutional archivist, you will often receive **new** series which form part of an existing **collection** (i.e., were created by the same department or agency as other records in the archives). In this case treat the new records as though they were a new series. In Step 12 you will link the two series in your finding aids by creating a subject card for the creator or compiler of each collection.

discover that they cover the years 1812-1910. One year later you receive a second group of birth records from the town clerk which date from 1911 to 1940. There are at least two ways to handle these new records (these records, by the way, are called an "accretion" to the earlier series of records).

The first way to handle an accretion is to assign a series number to the records and complete a series description sheet as if the new records had no relationship to the earlier series. In the content description section, however, you would write "see also series X" and refer the researcher to the content description of your earlier series. A second way of dealing with accretions is to assign the new records the same series number as the earlier records. This means that the earlier series description sheet must be rewritten and the new records placed on the shelf with the original series.

Step 10: Place the Collection Description Sheets and the Series Description Sheets in a Binder

Place the collection description sheet and the series description sheets in a three-ring binder with the collection sheet first, followed by the series sheets for each series in that collection.

Example: Figure 9 (page 27)

❖ **Explanation:** Now arrange your collection description sheets and your series description sheets in a three-ring binder. As the example in Figure 9 (page 27) shows, these should be arranged so that the collection description sheet for collection 1 is followed by the series description sheets of each series in that collection (1-1, 1-2, 1-3, etc.). These are followed by the collection description sheet for collection 2 and its series description sheets (2-1, 2-2, 2-3, etc.). As you add collections and series to your archives, just keep adding their description sheets to this binder. When the binder is full, get a second binder and keep going.

Step 11: Place the Containers on Shelves

Place the records on the shelves in the proper order. Either keep all records together or shelve by type of record (as described below).

❖ **Explanation:** You can put the containers (the boxes, volumes, etc.) on the shelves in a number of ways. The first way is to put everything together on the shelves; in other words, start at the first shelf and put the first item from the first series of the first collection (item 1-1.1) followed by the second item from that series (1-1.2) and so on until all of the items are on the shelf in numerical order. The advantage of this is that it makes it very easy to find anything you want by its item number. The disadvantage is that it takes a lot of shelf space — something that few of us have to spare.

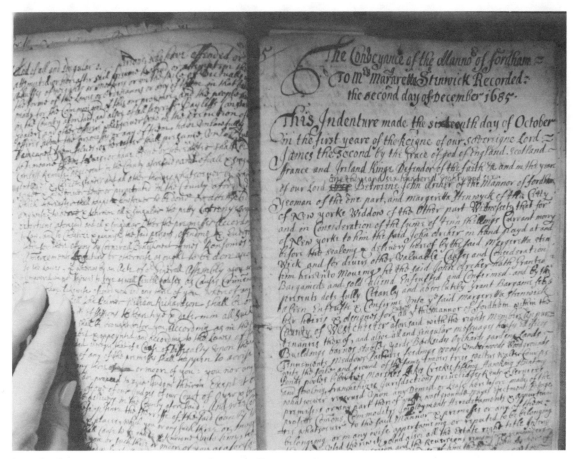

Bound volumes are an important part of many collections. Their proper care is essential to good archival practices. *(Photo: Diana Maull)*

A second method is to shelve like items together, that is, all of the bound volumes are shelved in one area of the archives, all of the boxes in another area, and so forth. This makes sense when you are shelving odd-sized materials like maps and photographs because it is much easier to store those kinds of materials together. If you shelve in this way, go ahead and shelve in numerical order, only skip numbers that belong to other formats. So, if item 1-1.1 is a bound volume, it is the first item on the shelf in the bound volumes section of the archives. If the next item (1-1.2) is a box, it becomes the first item in the boxes section of the archives. If item 1-1.3 is a box, it goes on the shelf next to 1-1.2. If item 1-1.4 is a bound volume, it goes on the shelf — in the bound volumes section — next to 1-1.1.

Using this method means that when a researcher asks for item 1-1.3 you may need to look several places in the archives for that item, but this should not pose too large a problem — and the advantage of saving space makes up for the disadvantage of looking two or three places for an item. If it becomes a big problem you may put a small letter after the item number in the container list to indicate where the item is shelved. For example, 1-1.1B could mean that item

1-1.1 is in the boxes ("B") section of the archives; 1-1.2V could be a bound volume ("V" for "volume"); "P" could be used for photographs and "M" for maps.

But, you may be saying to yourself, I thought I could not disturb the original order. If I don't shelve everything together, won't I be breaking up the original order? Separating items physically does not necessarily separate them intellectually. Once you have written your series description and carefully recorded the original order in the container list, you may separate the individual boxes or volumes and re-create the original order anytime by referring to your series description sheet.

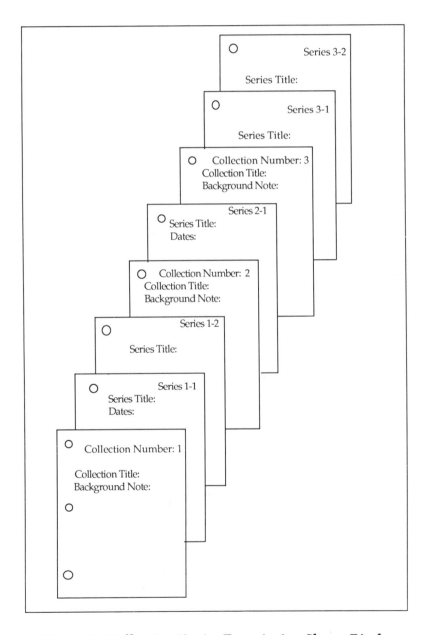

Figure 9: Collection/Series Description Sheets Binder

Step 12: Create Finding Aids

Write subject cards for the collection. Periodically produce a guide to all of the collections in your archives.

Example: Figures 10 and 11 (pages 28, 29)

❖ **Explanation:** Your final step is to create finding aids for this collection. Finding aids for a single collection take the form of catalog cards; for all of the collections in your archives, you may wish to produce a printed (or photocopied) guide. These are described below.

♦ **Catalog Cards:** Catalog cards, or subject cards, are the windows into each collection. The cards should be simple, like the ones shown in Figure 10, and give only the minimum information required to refer the researcher to the series description sheet. The researcher can then read the series description for more complete information about the records.

Once you have created catalog cards (which, by the way, need not be typed) you should file them alphabetically in a card drawer. The patron, then, looks in the card catalog for general subject headings, reads the series description sheets to get full information about the records, and then uses the container list at the bottom of each series description sheet to identify specific boxes or volumes to look at. This is illustrated in Figure 11 (page 29).

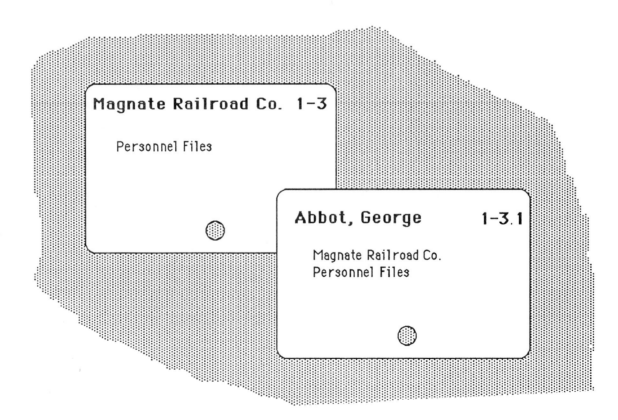

Figure 10: Subject Cards

There is much debate about subject headings: Should they come from the Library of Congress subject headings list? Should they come from the archivist's head? First, you should at least be aware that several accepted lists of subject headings are available in published form (the Library of Congress headings, the Sears headings, and a number of others).

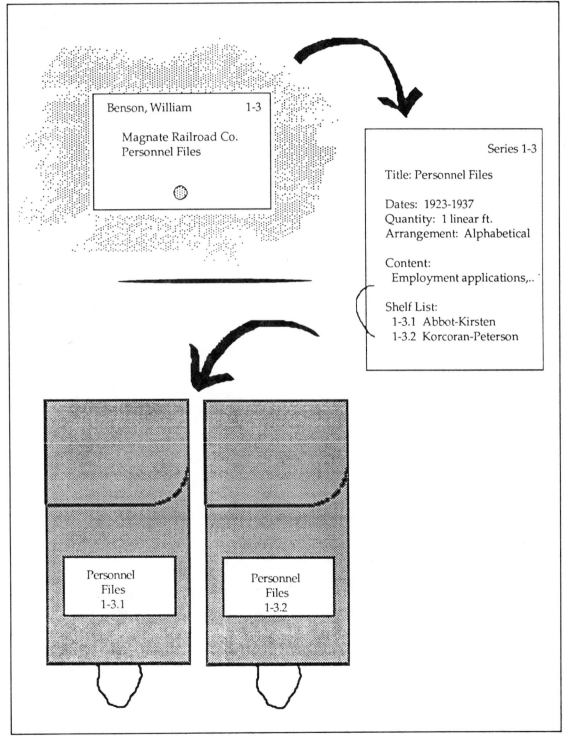

Figure 11: Retrieval Process

There are at least two advantages to using published sources: first, they are already there — you don't have to think up subject headings yourself. You just turn to the book and find an appropriate one. Second, if you ever want to share data with other institutions (by computer or even manually), the published subject headings lists give us a common language to use when speaking to one another. (Try, for example, going into an archives which uses the Library of Congress headings and looking for the items on the subject "World War I." You won't find anything because the proper heading is "World War, 1914-1918.")

As usual, there are disadvantages as well. First, the published subject heading lists were created for libraries and thus for books. This creates a problem for archives which is complex, but suffice it to say, the headings in published lists usually come close to describing the contents of archival materials but don't fit exactly.* The other drawback is that these subject heading lists are designed with national mega-collections in mind. The terms are often far too specific to be applied to small collections of local records.

The solution to this dilemma seems to be to use subject headings that work for you (published or local) and keep an "authority list." An authority list is simply a list of subject headings which you use in your archives. It is somewhat time consuming to keep such a list, but ultimately it will save much time. The purpose of the authority list is to establish what term you have chosen to use consistently to describe something (that way you won't use "World War, 1914-1918" one time and "World War I" the next time), and to minimize your work if your collection ever becomes so large that you want to convert your subject headings to those used in a published source. The importance of an authority list cannot be overemphasized. No good archives is without one.

You can create as many catalog cards for each collection as you want. Each collection must have a catalog card for the person or institution which created or compiled the collection. Such cards will link your collections by provenance.

♦ **Guides:** The advantage of a card catalog is that it can be updated easily — just add more cards. But its disadvantage is that it can't be mailed to researchers who live out of town. That's where collection guides come in. A guide does not need to be a fancy publication (a typewritten photocopied guide is fine), but it should always include the following elements:

  ♦ a brief overview of your archives (why it exists, where it is, when it is open to researchers, etc.)

  ♦ a short description of each collection (with its title, its quantity, and a short description of each of its series).

---

*This is primarily because libraries classify books on the basis of human knowledge while archives "classify" (if they can be said to classify at all) on the basis of human activity. The distinction is a fine one, but it shows up most clearly when you attempt to apply library subject headings to archival materials. Archivists are addressing this problem gradually through the use of functional terms, but you do not need to be concerned about that right now.

It is important for every archives to produce a guide and update it every few years. One of our key functions as archivists is to make material available to researchers. If our records are not used, they are useless. A guide is one of the most inexpensive means of advertising our collections, and it should be a top priority in every repository. For more information on guides and how to prepare them, see the works listed in the bibliography (page 50).

Now that you have finished Step 12, you have arranged and described your first collection. Congratulations! After you have read the concluding section you can follow Steps 1 through 12 for each collection you wish to arrange and describe. If you want more information on arrangement and description or on other archival topics, the bibliography lists further reading.

(Wharton Settlement Nursery 1938) Cataloging photographic resources provides valuable information for researchers. *(Photo: WPA Records, Pennsylvania State Archives)*

❖ CONCLUSION

The fact that you have read this manual shows that you are serious about making sense out of the records you are responsible for. But now that you've read it, there is always the possibility that you have more questions than you did before you started. In conclusion, then, let me make a few observations.

First, this method of arrangement and description is one way of doing things. It is not written in stone and it can be altered to fit specific needs. Certain principles, which I hope have been made clear, are more or less inviolable, but beyond these this manual should be used flexibly.

Secondly, the steps shown in "Steps of Organization," beginning on page 11, will probably merge with one another as you become more familiar with the process of arrangement and description. You may, for instance, create your finding aids while you are refoldering and boxing rather than as a separate step. The important thing is that you do all of the steps for each collection — and don't get so involved in one step that you don't have time to do the others.

And finally, arrangement and description are not as difficult as they appear. It boils down to getting records in a logical order (if possible, the order in which their creator arranged them) and then describing their content. If you can do that and then get things onto the shelf in such a way that they can be found when they are needed — and you can — then you have done your job.

Most of us do not deal every day with collections of national importance. We tend to have records which will be useful to local researchers, and occasionally to researchers interested in specific examples of national phenomena. This is good, because if from time to time we make a mistake in re-creating the original order of a collection, no one will probably ever know, much less care.

The most important thing is to roll up your sleeves and get started. Once you do, don't get sidetracked on any one collection. Some people like to index every collection, others like to put every piece of paper in perfect order; but to do so may mean spending precious time on one or two collections and never moving on to the dozens of others that deserve your attention.

In sum: do your best. Use this manual thoughtfully. If you get into a tight spot call someone for help. Your state archival agency is a good place to start. But, above all, just do it!

❖ APPENDIX

❖ RECORD AND MANUSCRIPT GROUPS

Because the primary purpose of this manual is to simplify the process of arrangement and description, a single term ("collections") has been selected to refer to groups of records in your archives which were created or compiled by a single source, regardless of whether that source was a person or an institution. You should be aware, however, that archivists make such a distinction and more often refer to records in their archives as "record groups" or "manuscript groups" rather than "collections." This section will introduce you to these terms in case you encounter them in other archival literature.

Archivists draw a technical distinction between "archives" (the historical records of an institution or organization) and "manuscripts" (the historical papers of an individual or family, or historical records created by businesses or organizations other than the repository's parent institution). This distinction leads to various practices which can be illustrated by imagining two repositories in the town of Centerville: the archives of the government of Centerville and the Centerville Historical Society.

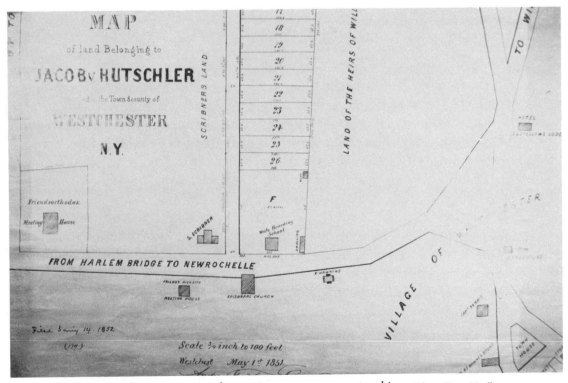

Maps can be an important element in many government archives. *(Photo: Diana Maull)*

The Archives of the government of Centerville is a true "archives" because it was established by an organization (the government of the town) to collect its own records. The Centerville Historical Society, on the other hand, is technically a "manuscript repository" because it was organized to collect personal papers ("manuscripts") of the town's citizens as well as records created by organizations other than its own parent organization (e.g., businesses and other non-government organizations in the town). In practice, of course, most people would refer to both of these repositories as "archives," but here we are concerned with the technical distinction between the two.

Centerville's government archives is a part of the government and collects records from its parent institution — from the mayor's office, the town clerk's office and other departments of the town government. As records are received at the archives they are grouped on the basis of who created them, in each case a department of the Centerville government. Thus, if the town clerk's office transfers a group of marriage licenses to the archives, the licenses are grouped with other records created or compiled by the town clerk's office. The records may not be grouped together physically, but they are "grouped" on paper, at least by means of lists.

Archivists call all of the records created by a single unit of the parent organization a "record group." In the case of a government, the "units" of the "parent organization" are usually the departments and offices which make up the government. This means that in the Centerville government archives all the records created or compiled by the town clerk's office form one record group — the town clerk's record group. And all of the records created or compiled by the mayor's office form another record group — the mayor's record group. The purpose of this is to keep the records created by one department or office separate from the records created by another.

Over at the Centerville Historical Society the concept is the same: do not mix records created by one person, family or business with those created by another, but the term "manuscript group" is used to refer to all the papers created by one person or group. The historical society will probably have many more manuscript groups than the archives has record groups. In the case of the former, almost every new group of records donated or purchased by the society will form a new manuscript group; but in the latter, almost every group of records transferred will be added to an existing record group. And while the historical society will usually receive whole manuscript groups at one time, the archives will frequently receive only portions of a record group at one time (most offices do not send all of their records to an archives at one time unless they are ceasing operations).

In actual practice the historical society may have both manuscript groups and record groups. If the society maintains the historical records of its own institution (e.g., the original charter of the historical society, the minutes of society meetings, etc.) it is, technically speaking, acting as the "archives" of the historical society. In fact, the society may even act as the official archives of some other organization in town and so have record groups from that organization as well. In the same way, the government archives may collect certain personal papers (e.g., the personal papers of the mayors of the town), and so may have manuscript groups in addition to its record groups.

Repositories handle their record groups and manuscript groups in various ways, but the important point is that the creator of the records is of primary importance in any archival collection. Archivists have emphasized this importance by developing the concept of record and manuscript groups.

In this manual we will refer to any group of records created by one person, family, business or agency as a "collection." Later, after you have become more familiar with arrangement and description theory and have read the more technical archival literature, you may decide that you would like to divide your collections into record groups and manuscript groups. If you have followed the steps in this manual carefully, you will be able to do so.

❖ EXERCISES AND ANSWERS

❖ Exercise A: Determining the creator/compilers of collections
(Answers begin on page 38.)

Instructions: A good collection title normally includes the name of the person or entity responsible for the collection's creation or compilation. On a separate sheet of paper give each of the collections below a title and include the name of the collection's creator or compiler in the title.

Collection 1 . . . Sixteen original handwritten letters, all signed by a local author, Meredith Emerson, and addressed to sixteen different people. These were in the archives before you arrived and there is no indication how they came to be there.

Collection 2 . . . Four maps of Newtown — one shows election districts, two are road maps, and one shows local bus routes — brought to the archives by Mark Hampton, who said that he picked them up at a local flea market and thought you might want them.

Collection 3 . . . This collection consists of four diaries (two belonging to Samantha Higgins and one each written by her husband George and her father William Merritt); four folders of correspondence (82 letters from George Higgins to his wife Samantha and 6 letters addressed to George from someone named Bertie); one high school yearbook with the name Samantha penciled in the front; and a photograph of George Higgins taken in Bermuda.

Collection 4 . . . Four hundred maps of Newtown. The maps date from 1812 to the present and were willed to the archives by the late Jonathan C. Murdock, who collected maps of Newtown all his life.

Collection 5 . . . Three diaries (one written by Sandra Scarponi and two by her brother Jimmy); sixteen photographs (10 of Sandra and six of Jimmy); fourteen letters to Bertha Scarponi (12 from her daughter Sandra and one each from her husband Lennie and her son Jimmy); one phonograph record inscribed "To my wife — happy 30th anniversary, Lennie." These records were in the archives before you arrived and there is no indication of where they came from.

❖ Answers to Exercise A

Collection 1 is tricky in that it is probable that someone other than the author of the letters compiled the letters (since each letter is addressed to a different recipient). If the letters were copies we could surmise that they were copies kept by the author for her own records. Since we do not know who compiled them, we are forced to call this the "Meredith Emerson Collection" — she being the person most closely associated with the records.

Did Mark Hampton create or compile **Collection 2?** Most archivists would probably say that he did not. He simply gathered them up and dropped them at the archives. There would be no harm in calling this the "Mark Hampton Collection" (if nothing else, it might impress the donor) but it might also be called the "Newtown Map Collection." On the other hand, many archives do not treat items such as these as a collection at all. Instead, if someone donates just a few maps (or photographs or postcards, etc.) which do not form part of a larger collection of records, the donation is recorded as an accession but the items are placed with other maps (or photographs or postcards) which have been donated in a similar manner. The archives is thus creating an "artificial collection" of maps. Note that maps which form part of a larger collection of records would not be removed from that collection to be placed in this artificial collection of maps. Artificial collections should be used only to deal with small donations such as the one described in this question.

It is very probable that **Collection 3** was the work of Samantha Higgins. The majority of the correspondence was received by her (and, thus, probably kept together by her), a majority of the diaries were hers, and the picture of her husband most likely belonged to her. The other items (her father's and husband's diaries, for example) are records which she might have collected for one reason or another. Although the collection could be called the "Higgins Family Papers," it is probably more correct to call it the "Samantha Higgins Papers."

Collection 4, unlike Collection 2, was systematically compiled by a single person, Jonathan C. Murdock. The proper title of this collection is the "Jonathan C. Murdock Map Collection."

Collection 5 has no clear compiler or creator. It is the work of the entire Scarponi family. The fact that more of the records were created by Sandra than by any other family member is not significant since there is no evidence that she compiled the other records in the collection. It should be called the "Scarponi Family Papers."

❖ Exercise B: Discovering series in collections
(Answers begin on page 40.)

Instructions: On a separate sheet of paper write down the series you would create out of the collection shown below. You have taken the materials from the box in the order shown below. Everything which was written on the outside of the folder or volume is indicated by bold type. The title of the collection is "Greeter Family Papers."

Lumber Invoices
6 folders containing carbon copies of invoices, each with the heading "Greeter Lumber Company" and signed by John or Laura Greeter; all invoices are dated between 1890 and 1900.

Lumber Invoices
13 folders containing carbon copies of invoices, each with the heading "Greeter Lumber Company" and signed by John or Laura Greeter; all invoices are dated between 1901 and 1910.

Correspondence
1 folder containing 34 letters from customers, all letters addressed to the "Greeter Lumber Company," all letters dated between 1896 and 1911.

John
1 folder containing 10 documents, all letters from John Greeter to Laura Greeter, 1890-1895.

1913
1 diary kept by Laura Greeter in the year 1913.

Adirondacks
1 folder containing 6 documents pertaining to a Boy Scout camping trip led by John Greeter in 1913.

Merit Badges
1 folder containing 3 documents, each related to boys earning merit badges in John Greeter's Boy Scout troop, 1914.

Training
1 folder containing 20 documents related to John Greeter's training as a Boy Scout leader in 1913.

❖ Answers to Exercise B

Remember that you are trying to discover the way the records were probably grouped when they were being used. The questions to ask yourself are, "What activity did these records relate to?" and "Are there other records which relate to this same activity?" Based on these questions, the records might be divided into the following series:

Series 1 . . . **Business Records**
Lumber Invoices, 1890-1900
Lumber Invoices, 1901-1910
[Business] Correspondence, 1896-1911

Series 2 . . . **Personal Papers**
John['s Correspondence], 1890-1895
[Diary of Laura Greeter], 1913

Series 3 . . . **Boy Scout Records**
[Boy Scouts], Adirondacks, 1913
[Boy Scouts], Merit Badges, 1914
[Boy Scouts], Training, 1913

Maintaining the family business is the activity reflected in Series 1. The records were probably kept together since they arrived at the archives in the order shown, and, in the case of the first two folders, their content is identical. If you wanted to become very specific you could divide these into two series — one for invoices and one for business correspondence. This is the manner in which many archivists would group the records, because this grouping more clearly emphasizes the separate activities involved in billing and corresponding. But in very small collections dividing records into many small series may lead to confusion. The fact is that the records have an activity in common (the family business) and their order suggests that the creators of the records kept them together, so putting these together in a single series makes sense.

The primary focus of the second series is the personal lives of the family as opposed to their business lives. We have no way of knowing whether these records were kept together by the family which created and compiled them, although the fact that they came into the archives in the order shown indicates that they may have been. The key is that generally they relate to the same activity and there is some chance that their creators kept them together. If there is any doubt, these two could be separated into two series, although this would again result in very small series. Note that the format of the records has nothing to do with whether they form a series or not. The bound volume belongs with the loose material on the basis of activity, not format.

The last series could conceivably be merged into Series 2 — it relates to the non-business aspect of the family. But the folders relate more specifically to a single activity: John Greeter's work with the Boy Scouts. Note that the folders were in alphabetical order when they came into the archives. If they had arrived in no discernible order you might have arranged them chronologically, but since they display an arrangement, you would leave the folders as you found them.

❖ **Exercise C:** Identifying collections, series and accessions
(Answers begin on page 42.)

Instructions: Circle the correct answer for each question below.

1. A group of records which were created or compiled by the same person, family, business, office or other entity is called a(n)
collection   series   accession.

2. When Mrs. Simpson donates three boxes of her grandmother's papers to your archives she has given you one
collection   series   accession.

3. The business correspondence in a large group of records from the Otis Frisbee Company Records is called a(n)
collection   series   accession.

4. A(n)   **collection   series   accession**   is a group of records which relate to the same activity or function.

5. When you are working with a group of records produced by the Widget family, you are working with a(n)   **collection   series   accession.**

6. A group of records donated to the archives together is called a(n)
collection   series   accession.

7. A set of twelve diaries in a group of records called the "Maria Benson Papers" may form one   **collection   series   accession.**

8. The title "Maria Benson Papers," in the example above, is the title of a(n)   **collection   series   accession.**

9. If you are looking at a group of records created by one person, you are looking at a(n)   **collection   series   accession.**

10. Every collection begins its life in your archives as a(n)
collection   series   accession
and is composed of one or more
collections   series   accessions.

❖ Answers to Exercise C

1. A group of records which were created or compiled by the same person, family, business, office or other entity is called a **collection.**

2. When Mrs. Simpson donates three boxes of her grandmother's papers to your archives she has given you one **accession.** (You should note that these papers constitute one collection if, indeed, they were all created or compiled by Mrs. Simpson's grandmother.)

3. The business correspondence in a large group of records from the Otis Frisbee Company Records is called a **series.**

4. A **series** is a group of records which relate to the same activity or function.

5. When you are working with a group of records produced by the Widget family, you are working with a **collection.**

6. A group of records donated to the archives together is called an **accession.**

7. A set of twelve diaries in a group of records called the "Maria Benson Papers" may form one **series.**

8. The title "Maria Benson Papers," in the example above, is the title of a **collection.**

9. If you are looking at a group of records created by one person, you are looking at a **collection.**

10. Every collection begins its life in your archives as an **accession** and is composed of one or more **series.**

❖ Exercise D: Creating artificial accessions
(Answers begin on page 44.)

Instructions: In Section 1 of this exercise you will find a list of five accession titles. In Section 2 are items which must be matched to their proper accession titles. In the box beside each item, write the number of the accession title it matches.

SECTION 1: Accession Titles
1. Wilson Family Papers
2. Johnson City High School Records
3. Gilson Guitar Company Records
4. Johnson City Government Records
5. Beekman Family Papers

SECTION 2: Items

☐ 1. Yearbook from Johnson City High School, 1954 — inscribed "Leonard Wilson"

☐ 2. Letter, dated 12 June 1956, from Margaret Chase to Meredith Wilson

☐ 3. Photo with inscription, "Gilson's International Headquarters, Grand Rapids, 1919"

☐ 4. Book entitled, "Record of Marriages — Johnson City," 1922-1934

☐ 5. Yearbook from Johnson City High School, 1919

☐ 6. Booklet entitled, "Rules for Faculty of Johnson City High School," 1961, inscribed "Leonard Wilson"

☐ 7. Folder entitled, "Gilson Guitar: Move to Michigan Headquarters," no date

☐ 8. Folder of photographs of the Beekman family, 1946-1961

☐ 9. Letter, dated 18 November 1959, from George Hammond to Leonard Wilson

☐ 10. Book of receipts from the Gilson Guitar Company, 1910-1943

☐ 11. Folder of correspondence between Marjorie Beekman and her daughters, 1950-1964

☐ 12. Map of Johnson City, 1926

☐ 13. Receipts from the Beekman Arms Hotel, 1953-1955

❖ Answers to Exercise D

Remember that when you are creating artificial accessions you are, in fact, creating artificial collections. This means that you are looking for records which were created or compiled by the same individual, family, organization, government, office or business. Each item must be placed in only one collection, even if it might logically be included in more than one. The items in the exercise might be grouped like this:

1. This item could be placed in either the "Wilson Family Papers" or the "Johnson City High School Records." It does not really matter which one you place it in, but you should try to determine if one is a more logical choice. If this book were on the shelf you could look at the items near it to determine whether they are Wilson family materials or items from the Johnson City High School.

2. This letter was received by Meredith Wilson — in other words, although she did not create the record, she added it to the compilation (or collected it). This belongs with the "Wilson Family Papers." Generally, **original letters belong in the collection of the person who received the letter; copies of letters belong in the collection of the person who sent the letter.**

3. The photo belongs with the "Gilson Guitar Company Records" because it was created or was among materials compiled by that company.

4. Marriage records are official government records; this is why a separate "Johnson City Government Records" collection was created. A case could be made that all of the Johnson City records should be placed together, but consider this: since "collections" are groups of records created or compiled by a single person or group of people, the best collection titles contain the name of the creator or compiler of the records. Thus, "Johnson City High School Records" and "Johnson City Government Records" indicate that one collection was created by one organization (the high school) while the other collection was created by another organization (the government). In both cases, the title makes it clear that a limited number of people were involved in creating or compiling the collection (people associated with the high school and the government). Merging the two collections produces a title ("The Johnson City Records") without a specific creator.

5. Place this with the "Johnson City High School Records." You might think, at first, that this belongs to Leonard Wilson (since he owned the yearbook in item 1), but since this yearbook is dated 1919 and item 1 is dated 1954, it is unlikely that they belong to the same person.

6. See the notes under item 1. They apply to this item as well.

7. This item probably goes with item 3 and belongs in the "Gilson Guitar Company Records."

8. This is the first item belonging to the Beekman Family and is the first item in the "Beekman Family Papers" collection. You may have noticed by now that some titles use the word "papers" while others use the word "records." The first word (papers) is used to refer to records of private individuals or families. The second (records) refers to businesses, governments and other organizations. If you can replace these two words with a more specific word (such as "correspondence," "minutes," "invoices," etc.) you should do so.

9. The rule spelled out in item 2 applies here; this item belongs in the "Wilson Family Papers."

10. The "Gilson Guitar Company Records."

11. "Beekman Family Papers."

12. This probably belongs in one of the two Johnson City collections. Here you must use your judgment (remember, you won't be arrested for making a mistake).

13. Probably the Beekman Arms Hotel was owned by the Beekman Family (you would check the records themselves for clues). If so, place these with the "Beekman Family Papers."

❖ Exercise E: Arranging items within a series

(Answers begin on page 47.)

Instructions: Below you will find three series titles. After each title is a list of five items in the series. Place the items in each series in order using the boxes provided to write a number 1 beside the item which would come first in the series, a 2 beside the item which would come next, and so on. Note that the series themselves have no relationship to one another.

Series title: Diaries of Evelyn DeNito

☐ 1910-1912

☐ 1921-1930

☐ 1913-1917

☐ 1917-1922

☐ 1931-1960

Series title: Marriage Licenses

☐ Lic. #6840, 11/10/34, William Everett - Janice Carnes

☐ Lic. #6842, 11/12/34, John Baxter - Margaret Reeve

☐ Lic. #6902, 02/03/35, Bruce Kinde - Beth Cline

☐ Lic. #4006, 06/06/32, Kelly O'Brian - Sylvia Denver

☐ Lic. #7321, 08/26/35, Brian McGinty- Yvonne Flanders

Series title: Wills

☐ Affle, Johnny-1819:2

☐ Abbot, Marilyn - 1819:1

☐ Bork, Roger - 1819:3

☐ Bass, David - 1820:2

☐ Acton, Laura - 1820:1

❖ Answers to Exercise E

The series should probably be arranged as follows:

Series title: Diaries of Evelyn DeNito

> 1910-1912
> 1913-1917
> 1917-1922
> 1921-1930
> 1931-1960

The arrangement here is chronological, although the third and fourth items overlap for some reason. This small inconsistency is not enough to disrupt the overall chronological order.

Series title: Marriage Licenses

> Lic.#4006, 06/06/32, O'Brian-Denver
> Lic.#6840, 11 /10/34, Everett-Carnes
> Lic.#6842, 11 /12/34, Baxter-Reeve
> Lic.#6902, 02/03/35, Kinde-Cline
> Lic.#7321, 08/26/35, McGinty-Flanders

If you were tempted to put these in alphabetical order but did not, give yourself a pat on the back. The numerical order shown above makes sense because government offices often keep these types of records in some sort of numerical order. When you add the fact that putting them in numerical order also results in a chronological arrangement, it seems likely that this was the original order of the records. Resist the temptation to put everything in alphabetical order! If you get a collection of 10,000 such records and put them all in alphabetical order by the name of the groom, two things will happen: the first ten researchers through the door will remember only the name of the bride, and an index to the records will be found one week after you finish the rearrangement. Guaranteed!

Series title: Wills

> 1819:1 - Abbot, Marilyn
> 1819:2 - Affle, Johnny
> 1819:3 - Bork, Roger
> 1820:1 - Acton, Laura
> 1820:2 - Bass, David

The same rules (and the same guarantees) apply here as applied to the marriage records in the series before. It is obvious from this arrangement that the office kept its records alphabetically, but started over each year. The system worked for them, it will work for you.

❖ Exercise F: Arranging series within a collection
(Answers begin on page 49.)

Instructions: Below are series titles from two collections. Place the series titles in order using the boxes provided to write a number 1 beside the title which would come first in the collection, a 2 beside the title which would come next, and so on. The collections have no relationship to one another.

Collection Title: Records of the Smith Widget Company

☐   Minutes of the Board of Directors, 1915-1957

☐   Correspondence of President John Smith, 1906-1942

☐   Contracts and Specifications, 1915-1960

☐   Building Plans, 1954

☐   Agenda of the Board of Directors, 1915-1960

☐   Minutes of the Building Committee, 1952

Collection Title: Records of the Richland Town Clerk

☐   Birth Records 1860-1910

☐   Death Certificates, 1892-1926

☐   Laws of the Richland Town Board, 1899-1940

☐   Marriage Licenses, 1875-1930

☐   Marriage License Applications, 1874-1922

☐   Minutes of the Richland Town Board, 1899-1903

☐   Index to Birth Records, 1860-1910

❖ Answers to Exercise F

The arrangement of series within a collection is a result of individual preference, knowledge and judgment. The suggested answers to this exercise are explained below.

Collection Title: Records of the Smith Widget Company

Agenda of the Board of Directors
Minutes of the Board of Directors

Correspondence of President John Smith

Minutes of the Building Committee
Contracts and Specifications
Building Plans

I have grouped the series to help explain their order. The various series related to the board of directors come first because the board of directors comes first in the company hierarchy. The agenda are put before the minutes simply because the agenda come first in time — they must be prepared in advance of each board meeting while the minutes are produced after each meeting.

The president's records come next because, after the board of directors, he is the highest official in the company.

The remaining records all relate to building construction. The minutes of the committee which oversees construction are placed first because of their authority over the process. Next come the contracts and then the building plans in this order because of their place in the process itself (contracts must be written before plans are drawn up, so the contracts and specifications have priority of time).

Collection Title: Records of the Richland City Clerk

Minutes of the Richland Town Board
Laws of the Richland Town Board

Index to Birth Records
Birth Records

Marriage License Applications
Marriage Licenses
Death Certificates

The board's series are placed first because they represent the highest authority in the collection. The order here is not important.

Next come birth, marriage and death records — placed in this order because they occur in this order. The index to birth records is placed first only because archivists traditionally place indexes just before the records they index. The marriage applications come before the licenses, again because that is the order in which the events occur.

❖ BIBLIOGRAPHY

The seven books listed below are intended for those who wish to read further about specific topics. Obviously many more books and articles could have been included, but these seven are recommended as basic reference tools for the small archives.

General Work . . . . Pederson, Ann. *Keeping Archives.* Sydney: Australian Society of Archivists, Inc., 1987.

Arrangement and Description . . . . *Guidelines for Arrangement and Description of Archives and Manuscripts: A Manual for Historical Records Programs in New York. State.* Albany: The University of the State of New York, 1991.

Miller, Fredric M. *Arranging and Describing Archives and Manuscripts.* Chicago: Society of American Archivists, 1990.

Conservation . . . . Ritzenthaler, Mary Lynn. *Archives & Manuscripts: Conservation.* Chicago: Society of American Archivists, 1983.

Government Records . . . . Dearstyne, Bruce W. *The Management of Local Government Records: A Guide for Local Officials.* Nashville: American Association for State and Local History Press, 1988.

Libraries . . . . Thompson, Enid T. *Local History Collections: A Manual for Librarians.* Nashville: American Association for State and Local History, 1978.

Photographs . . . . Ritzenthaler, Mary Lynn; Munoff, Gerald J.; and Long, Margery S. *Archives & Manuscripts: Administration of Photographic Collections.* Chicago: Society of American Archivists, 1984.

❖ INDEX

A

Accession date 7, 9
Accession number:
   cross-referencing 13
   defined 7
Accession sheet. 7, 8
Accessions:
   artificial 9, 43-45
   defined. 6-7, 41-42
   numbering. 7, 9, 13
   registering. 7-9
   shelving. 8, 25-27
Archives, comparison to manuscripts. 33-35
Arrangement and description:
   emphasis of 2, 23
   purpose of. 1, 32
Authority list 30

B

Background note:
   content of 14-16
   example 15
   sources of 16
Books, comparison to archival records 1-2

C

Collection description sheet 12, 15, 17-18, 25
Collection number 12-13
Collection title 16, 36-37
Collections:
   artificial 9, 43-45
   conservation work on. 13-14
   creator or compiler of. 3-4, 11, 15-16, 30, 36-38
   creator or compiler unknown. 4, 38
   defined 3-4, 7, 33, 41-42
   examining. 13
   numbering 12-13
   title 3-4, 16

Conservation 13-14
Containers: 14
    numbering. 19-21, 25-27
    retrieval of 28-29
    shelving. 8, 25-27

D

Donor information 7

F

Finding aids 18, 28-31, 32

G

Guide to collections 30-31

I

Indexing archival records 1, 17-18, 32
Items, numbering. 20-21

L

Libraries, comparison to archives. 1-2, 30

M

Manuscript groups 33-35
Manuscript repositories 33-35
Manuscripts, comparison to archives 33-35

O

Original order, sanctity of 17, 25, 27, 32

P

Papers, use of the term 45
Provenance, principle of. 9, 30

R

Record groups 33-35
Records, use of the term 33-35, 45
Retrieval of containers 28

S

Series:
    accretions (additions) to 24-25
    arranging in relation to other series 19, 48-49
    arranging records within 18-19, 20, 23, 46-47
    clues to existence of 5
    container list 23
    content description 23
    dates 23
    defined 4-6, 39-42
    discovering in a collection 4-6, 17, 39-41
    numbering 19-21
    title 23
    quantity 23
Series description sheet 22-25, 28
Subject cards 28, 30
Subject headings 28-30

T

Titles:
    accession 7
    collection 16
    series 23

W

Work area 11